kijc

Legendary Nonfiction CRAFTS

by Marne Ventura

4D™

An Augmented Reading Crafting Experience

CAPSTONE PRESS

a capstone imprint

Dabble Lab Books are published by Capstone Press,
1710 Roe Crest Drive
North Mankato, Minnesota 56003

www.mycapstone.com

Library of Congress Cataloging-in-Publication Data
Names: Ventura, Marne, author.
Title: Legendary nonfiction crafts : 4D an augmented reading crafting
  experience / by Marne Ventura.
Description: North Mankato, Minnesota : Capstone Press, 2018. | Series:
  Dabble lab. Next chapter crafts 4D | Audience: Ages 6-10.
Identifiers: LCCN 2017040763 (print) | LCCN 2017045839 (ebook) | ISBN
  9781543506914 (eBook PDF) | ISBN 9781543506877 (hardcover)
Subjects: LCSH: Handicraft—Juvenile literature. | Children—Books and
  reading—Juvenile literature.
Classification: LCC TT160 (ebook) | LCC TT160 .V455 2018 (print) | DDC
  745.5—dc23
LC record available at https://lccn.loc.gov/2017040763

Editorial Credits
Mari Bolte, editor; Lori Bye, designer; Morgan Walters, media researcher;
Kathy McColley, production specialist

Photo Credits: All photographs by Capstone Studio/Karon Dubke except:
Shutterstock: Art Alex, 19, CkyBe, design element throughout, Neti.OneLove, design
element throughout

Printed and bound in the USA.
010760S18

TABLE OF CONTENTS

Books are the Best!

Identify the cool rock you found. Learn to paint. Find out about life in Asia, Australia, or Africa. Explore the solar system. Informational books help you follow your interests, try out new skills, and discover the world.

Use this book to make arts and crafts based on your favorite subjects. Many of the supplies needed are items you might already have in your home. If not, you can find them at dollar stores, discount department stores, and craft shops.

Are you ready to get started? Just read over the directions, gather up your supplies and begin. Feel free to improvise and come up with your own ideas too.

Download the Capstone 4D app!

- Ask an adult to search in the Apple App Store or Google Play for "Capstone 4D".
- Click Install (Android) or Get, then Install (Apple).
- Open the app.
- Scan any of the following spreads with this icon:

When you scan a spread, you'll find fun extra stuff to go with this book! You can also find these things on the web at *www.capstone4D.com* using the password: ncc.nonfiction

ROCK HOUND
BOOK BOX

Sedimentary, igneous, or metamorphic—rocks are beautiful. Rock hounds need a cool place to show off their treasures. Upcycle a hardbound book into a handy storage case.

What You'll Need:

craft knife
hardbound book
15 half-sheets of
    craft foam
ruler
pen
scissors
white glue
hot glue
self-adhesive
    magnets
label maker (or
    strips of white
    paper and
    pen)
cardstock

Steps:

1. Ask an adult to cut the pages from the book with the craft knife.

2. Center one sheet of foam on the inside of the back cover. Attach with white glue. Let it dry completely.

3. Measure and mark ¾-inch (2 centimeters) in from the edges of the remaining foam sheets. Ask an adult help you cut away the center rectangle. Discard the rectangles, or save them for another project.

4. Glue the frames, one at a time, to the sheet of foam in the back cover. Let the glue dry completely before adding the next.

5. Use hot glue to attach the spine to the side of the foam. Use additional glue along the edge where the spine and foam attach.

6. Stick a self-adhesive magnet to the inside cover. Stick another to the foam. This will keep your book closed.

7. Arrange your rocks inside the book. Hot glue them in place.

8. Add labels underneath each rock type.

9. Print and cut out fact cards.

10. Cut out a piece of cardstock that's 1 inch (2.5 cm) longer and wider than the fact cards. Fold in three edges of the cardstock 1/2 inch (1.2 cm).

11. Glue the folded edges of the cardstock to the inside lid of the book. Let the glue dry completely before sliding in the fact cards.

3.

5.

9.

NOW TRY THIS!

Skip hot gluing the rocks and use your book for everyday storage instead.

ARACHNID ART

There are between 35,000 and 40,000 species of spiders around the world. Don't be scared! Celebrate these cool creatures in art instead.

What You'll Need:

pencil
round canvas panel
white glue
paintbrush
watercolor paints
table salt
black or silver puffy paint
glue
googly eyes

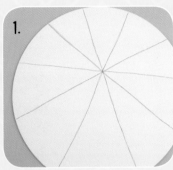

Steps:

1. Make light pencil marks to draw a spider web onto the canvas panel.

2. Trace the spider web with white glue. Let the glue dry completely.

3. Brush the entire canvas with a thin coat of water. Dip your brush in more water before brushing on shades of blue, green and purple paint.

4. Sprinkle salt onto the wet paint. Let the canvas dry completely.

5. Carefully brush the salt off the canvas.

6. Add a spider with the puffy paint. Let the paint dry completely.

7. Glue on googly eyes.

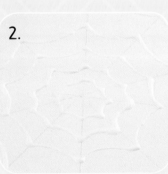

NOW TRY THIS!

Experiment with different paint supplies or techniques. How does the salt and paint look when you use watercolor paper? Try different types of paper too. What happens when you sprinkle salt onto the wet glue, and then paint the salt?

GLOBAL MATCH-UP

Have fun with geography and learn the names of new places.
Recycle maps, almanacs, or geography books into game
pieces. Match up the places you've visited and the ones
you hope to see some day.

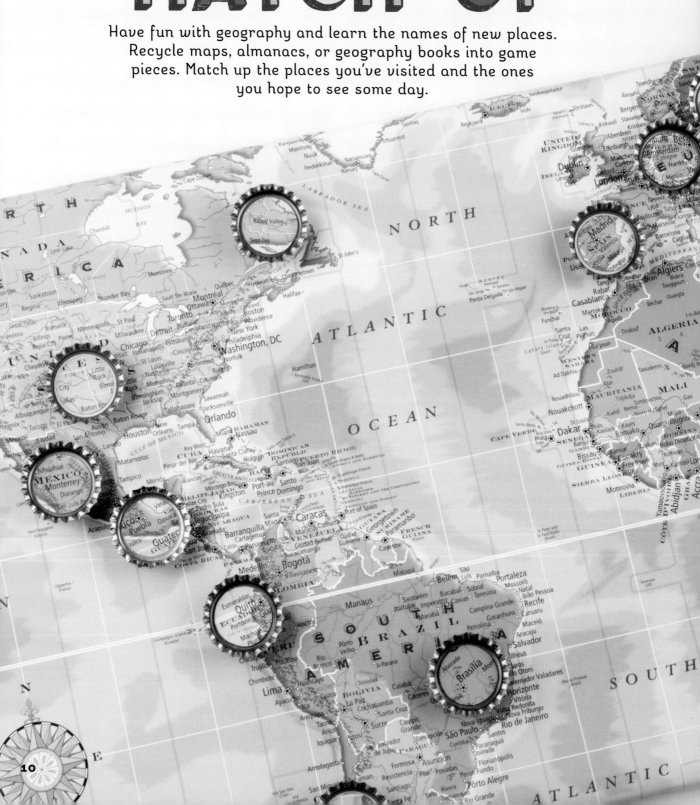

What You'll Need:

two copies of the same
    map or atlas page
bottle caps
pencil

scissors
white glue
self-adhesive magnets
magnetic white board

Steps:

1. Find large cities, capitols, or other interesting destinations on the map.

2. Use a bottle cap to trace circles over your chosen locations. Cut them out.

3. Glue the circles to the inside of the bottle caps. Let the glue dry completely.

4. Stick the magnets to the backs of the bottle caps.

5. Tape the corners of the second map so it covers the white board.

6. Turn the bottle caps face down. Take turns flipping them over, one at a time. Place the bottle cap in the correct location on the map.

7. The player who turns over the most bottle caps wins!

2.

3.

4.

NOW
TRY THIS!

Don't feel limited to maps! You can play this game many different ways:

- **Civil War:** Cut out pictures of Union and Confederate leaders. Place a United States map onto the white board. Which general goes where? Who won which battle?
- **Famous Places:** Match pictures of famous places, such as the Taj Mahal, Eiffel Tower, and Hoover Dam, to their home country.
- **Dino Wars:** Make a two-columned chart and divide dinos into meat eaters and plant eaters. Or turn the white board into a timeline, and place the dinos in the right time periods.

STITCHED
BASEBALL

Baseballs used in Major League games must have 108 stitches. They're always sewn by hand. Yours might not have that many, but you'll still have a hand-stitched baseball when you're done.

What You'll Need:

1 yard (0.9 meters) green felt
12-inch (20.5-cm) square cork board tile
craft glue
6 inch (15.2 cm) plastic lid
book page
pencil

scissors
awl, or hammer and 8-penny (2-inch) nail
red embroidery floss and embroidery needle
cardstock in two colors
hot glue and hot glue gun

Steps:

1. Cut the felt to cover the cork board. Glue into place.

2. Set the plastic lid onto the book page. Trace and cut out the circle.

3. Overlap the plastic lid over about 1/3 of the circle. Trace lightly along the edge to make a stitch line. Repeat on the other side of the circle.

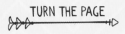

TURN THE PAGE

4. Make a pencil mark every ¼-inch (0.6-cm) along each stitch line. Then draw two angled ¼-inch lines from each mark.

5. Carefully hammer the nail into each pencil mark to make holes. Make holes on the ends of the angled lines too.

6. Cut a 3-foot (1-m) length of embroidery thread. Knot one end, and thread the needle onto the other.

7. Start at the end of an angled line. Push the needle from the back of the paper to the front. Then send the needle back through the nearest hole in the stitch line.

8. Repeat step 7 with the other angled line.

Use your baseball board to display playing cards, tickets, stats, or other fun baseball memorabilia!

9. Continue stitching until the entire curve is covered. Tie a knot and cut off any excess thread.

10. Repeat for the curve on the other side.

11. Cut out a burst shape from the cardstock. Make sure the burst is large enough to be seen behind the baseball.

12. Use the burst as a template to make a second burst in another color.

13. Slightly overlap the bursts, and then glue them together. Then glue them onto the felt-covered cork board.

14. Center the baseball over the bursts. Then glue them together.

NOW
TRY THIS!

Instead of felt, use decoupage glue to decorate the corkboard with old baseball cards.

PAPER
PLANETARIUM

Celebrate the solar system with a mobile model of the sky.
Make one model of your favorite planet, or go all-out and
display the entire galaxy.

What You'll Need:

scissors
old book paper
green and blue colored paper
glue
colored paper in yellows, oranges,
    blues, reds, and greens
clear fishing line
hot glue and hot glue gun
wooden sticks
string

Steps:

1. Start with Earth. Cut out three 3-inch (7.6 cm) circles from the old book paper.

2. Cut out two 3-inch circles from the blue paper.

3. Cut out two 3-inch circles from the green paper.

4. Fold all the circles in half.

5. Glue one outside edge of a half circle to another circle's outside edge.

6. Repeat step 5 until all the half circles are glued together and you have a sphere shape. Aternate between book paper and colored paper.

TURN THE PAGE

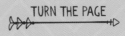

9.

10.

11.

13.

7. Repeat steps 1-6 for the remaining planets. Cut circles in various sizes, depending on how large or small the planet is. Use different colors too.

8. To make Saturn's rings, cut out a 4-inch (10.2 cm) circle.

9. Cut a 3-inch slit across the center of the paper. Then make two more, to make a star shape.

10. Slide the circle over Saturn until it's centered on the planet.

11. To hang each planet, cut a long length of fishing line. Carefully add a dab of hot glue into the top of a planet. Then quickly push one end of the fishing line into the glue. Let the glue dry completely.

12. Repeat until all the planets have fishing line.

13. Cross the wooden sticks at their middles to make an X shape. Wrap string around the middle to secure the X, and tie the ends.

14. Loop and tie another piece of string around the middle. This will be how you hang your solar system.

15. Tie the planets' strings to the sticks. Vary the height and distance between each planet.

16. When you're pleased with how your planets look, use the long string attached to the sticks to display your universe.

FOLLOW THIS COLOR CHART TO CREATE YOUR SOLAR SYSTEM!

Venus: gold, orange, and brown

Mercury: gray, brown, and white

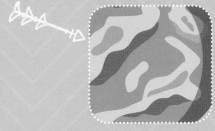

Mars: shades of red

Earth: blue and green

Saturn: light yellow, gold, and tans

Jupiter: orange and shades of brown

Uranus: shades of light blue

Neptune: shades of dark blue

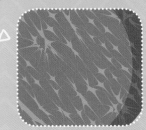

NOODLE
DOODLE

Real or fictional, big or small, robots are amazing! You can make your own with just a few basic parts. Then watch this tiny 'droid as it spins and draws circles.

1.

3.

5.

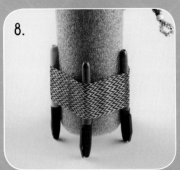

8.

What You'll Need:

craft knife
foam pool noodle
spray paint
spray adhesive
glitter
battery-powered
    toothbrush
hot glue and hot
    glue gun

googly eyes
chenille stem
plastic beads
markers
rubber bands
colored or
    patterned
    duct tape
paper

Steps:

1. Ask an adult to cut the noodle the same length as the toothbrush.

2. When the paint is dry, spray both ends of the noodle with adhesive. Dip the glued ends in glitter. Tap to remove any extra glitter.

3. Push the toothbrush into the noodle. The toothbrush's base and on/off switch should extend about ½-inch (1.3-cm) out the top of the noodle.

4. Press the googly eyes into the top of the noodle. Use hot glue to hold them in place.

5. Cut a chenille stem in half. Thread beads onto the stems.

6. Poke one end of a stem into the noodle. Curve the other end into a hand. Repeat for the second stem.

7. Space five markers evenly around the noodle. The ink ends should extend about an inch (2.5 cm) past the bottom of the noodle. Secure with two rubber bands.

8. Hide the rubber bands with duct tape.

9. Remove the marker caps. Set the robot on a sheet of paper. Then hit the on switch and let your robot loose!

OCEAN LIFE MOSAIC

Use magazine-quality photos (from where else—a magazine!) to celebrate the beauty of marine life in a mosaic.

What You'll Need:

pencil
6 inch (15.3 cm) square canvas
wildlife or outdoor magazine
scissors
colored paper
paintbrush
decoupage glue

Steps:

1. Lightly draw a fish design onto the canvas.

2. Flip through the magazine to find photos in the colors you want to use for the fish. Ask an adult if you can cut up the pages. Cut the pages into small squares, triangles, and other geometric shapes. Cut smaller pieces to use as space filler, as needed.

3. Cut up colored paper for the ocean background.

4. Arrange the paper pieces on the canvas.

5. Use a paintbrush to lay a thin layer of decoupage glue on the canvas. Press the photo squares into the glue. Work section by section, to keep the glue from drying out too soon.

6. Continue until you have covered the entire canvas. Fill any bare spots with the smaller pieces of magazine paper.

7. Find articles in the magazine that you like. Cut them out in circles of varying sizes. Arrange them on the canvas to resemble bubbles coming from the fish's mouth. Glue them into place.

8. Paint a thin layer of decoupage glue over the entire surface. Let dry completely.

NOW TRY THIS!

Try this with other art supplies! Fabric strips, construction paper, or even real photos would work. Use a little bit of everything!

THE
STORY OF ME

Tales about world leaders, civil rights activists, artists, and scientists are fascinating. Their stories have been told and bound into books. No one can read your story if you don't print it! Will you follow the footsteps of Abe Lincoln, Malala Yousafzai, Pablo Picasso, or Marie Curie?

1.

2.

3.

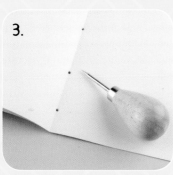

5.

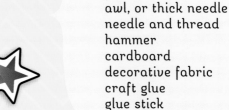

What You'll Need:

- plain paper
- ruler
- pencil
- awl, or thick needle
- needle and thread
- hammer
- cardboard
- decorative fabric
- craft glue
- glue stick

Steps:

1. Stack 5 pieces of paper. Fold the stack in half the short way. Crease the fold. This is called a signature. Repeat until you have as many signatures as you want. Use different colored paper for each signature, if desired.

2. Open one signature. Use a ruler to measure and a pencil to mark four light dots evenly along the crease.

3. With an adult's help, use the awl to punch a hole through each mark.

4. Repeat steps 2 and 3 with the remaining signatures.

5. Thread the needle through the holes in one signature. Start at one end, from the outside in. Pull the needle up through the second hole, and down through the third hole. Keep sewing until you reach the last hole. Pull the thread tight.

TURN THE PAGE

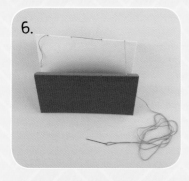

6. Line signature 2 up with signature 1. Push the needle and thread down through the closest hole in signature 2. This will sew the signatures together.

7. Bring the needle and thread up through the second hole of signature 2. Then thread it down through the second hole of signature 1. Thread it up through the next hole in signature 1, and then down through the same hole in signature 2. Finish threading signature 2.

8. When you've added all your signatures, pull the thread tight. Tie it off by looping it around the second-to-last signature loop. Make a good knot, and cut, leaving about a ½-inch (1.3-cm) tail. Use binder clips to hold the signatures in place.

9. To make the cover, measure and cut two pieces of cardboard that are 1/8-inch (0.3-cm) longer and wider than your book.

10. Measure and cut a piece of cardboard the same length and width as your signature's binding.

11. Set the fabric on your workspace, with the nice side down. Place the cardboard onto the paper. The binding piece should be in the middle, with a little room on either side. Cut the paper, leaving a ½-inch border all the way around.

12. Use craft glue to attach the fabric to the cardboard.

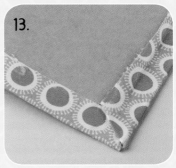

13. Fold the fabric up and use the craft glue to attach it along the edges of the cardboard. Crease the folds well.

14. Place the signatures inside the cover. Attach the first page of the signatures to the inside cover. This will be the front end page.

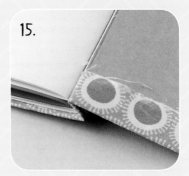

15. Use craft glue along the spine to attach the binding to the pages' spine. Press the two pieces together well.

16. Attach the back end page with the glue stick. Then close the book.

17. Use binder clips along the three non-spine edges to keep the book securely closed until the glue dries.

18. Glue a picture of yourself on the front cover. Use scrapbooking supplies to add embellishments!

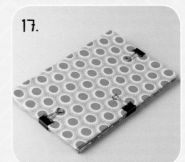

NOW TRY THIS!

Making the book was hard. Filling it could be even harder! Use some of these writing prompts to get inspired.

- Gather your own history! Start with the easiest. When were you born, and where? What's your favorite food? Do you have a favorite book? Where would you visit if you could go anywhere?

- Dream of adventure! Write a fictional story, but make it about you. Put yourself in the Old West, or on the moon. Are you an explorer or a survivor?

BEANBAG BOCCE

Bocce is an ancient game. Players try to toss special balls toward a smaller ball, called a jack. The team that gets their balls closest to the jack wins. Play an easier—and safer!—indoor version with these beanbags. The winning shot will help you decide what book to read next.

1.

2.

3.

5.

6.

What You'll Need:

ruler
scissors
fat quarter of cotton fabric
needle and thread (or sewing machine)
½ cup (120 milliliters) rice
paper and markers
six 18-ounce (0.5 liter) plastic cups
hot glue and hot glue gun
large, heavy book

Steps:

1. Measure and cut an 8-by-4-inch (20.3-by-10.2 cm) rectangle of fabric.

2. Place the fabric rectangle right-side-up on your work station. Then fold the rectangle in half, with the short sides touching.

3. Sew along the top and left side of the fabric.

4. Turn the fabric right-side-out.

5. Fill the fabric with rice.

6. Fold the edges of the fabric's open side in ¼ of an inch (0.6 cm). Pin the edges together so that the center of each side becomes a corner. Hand-sew, using small stitches.

TURN THE PAGE

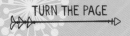

29

7.

7. Make labels for six of your favorite book subjects. You could also choose six books you've been wanting to read, but haven't. Place one label in each cup.

8. Hot glue the base of the cups to the book. The book will keep the cups upright and stable while you play.

9. Stand back a few feet and toss the beanbag. The cup that ends up with the most beanbags holds the book you'll read next!

NOW TRY THIS!

Traditional bocce ball sets come with eight balls in two colors. Make a full set of beanbags. Use just two colors, or get crazy with prints! Play for points instead of book subjects.

Can't decide what to do your book report on? Not sure what project to pick for the science fair? Let the Bocce beanbags decide! Just replace the book subjects with whatever topic you need to choose.

CHECK OUT ALL OF THE NEXT CHAPTER CRAFTS SERIES!

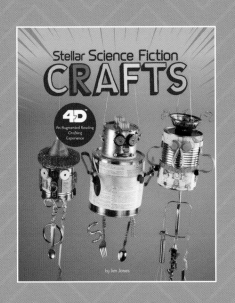

READ MORE

Braden, Linda Z. *Mason Jar Crafts for Kids: More Than 25 Cool, Crafty Projects to Make for Your Friends, Your Family, and Yourself!* New York: Sky Pony Press, 2015.

Galat, Joan Marie. *Maker Projects for Kids Who Love Printmaking.* New York: Crabtree Publishing Company, 2017.

MAKERSPACE TIPS

Download tips and tricks for using this book and others in a library makerspace.

Visit www.capstonepub.com/dabblelabresources

INTERNET SITES

Use FactHound to find Internet sites related to this book.

Visit www.facthound.com

Just type in 9781543506877 and go.